PROJECT MANAGEMENT

QuickStart Guide

Th...   ...er's
Guid...   ...ement

ClydeBank | BUSINESS

D1615572

Edition # 1 – Updated : April 27, 2016

Cover Illustration and Design: Katie Poorman, Copyright © 2016 by ClydeBank Media LLC
Interior Design: Katie Poorman, Copyright © 2016 by ClydeBank Media LLC

ClydeBank Media LLC
P.O Box 6561
Albany, NY 12206
Printed in the United States of America

Copyright © 2016
ClydeBank Media LLC
www.clydebankmedia.com
All Rights Reserved

ISBN-13 : 978-1-945051-07-4

contents

INTRODUCTION 7

| 1 | THE TRADITIONAL APPROACH 9

    Project Initiation 10

    Project Planning 11

    Project Execution 13

    Project Monitoring & Controlling 15

    Project Closing 17

    Why Projects Fail 17

| 2 | THE CRITICAL CHAIN APPROACH 21

    The Theory of Constraints 21

    The Critical Chain Process 23

    Criticisms 26

| 3 | BENEFITS REALIZATION MANAGEMENT 29

    Criticisms 32

| 4 | EARNED VALUE MANAGEMENT 33

    Criticisms 37

| 5 | AGILE PROJECT MANAGEMENT 39

    The 12 Principles of Agile Project Management 41

    Scrum 43

    Criticism 46

CONCLUSION 49

ABOUT CLYDEBANK 51

Feel free to take notes beginning on page 52.

introduction

The business world has always been a reflection of needs. Fulfilling needs, creating needs, identifying needs; these activities form the very basic roots of how economies operate and how business organizations function. Business needs and the needs of customers are addressed through day-to-day activities, but when normal operations aren't enough a solution is required. This is the role of the project: to organize and unify efforts to reach a common and specific goal. This is certainly an "easier said than done" scenario; large-scale projects can include mammoth investments and the coordination of hundreds of people. When handled effectively and efficiently, however, a well-executed project can move mountains (in the case of mining and mineral extraction, quite literally).

As the business environment becomes more complex, organizations are finding themselves increasingly in need of competent and effective project managers, people who have an attention to detail but a big-picture perspective. This may sound contradictory, but project management can be an enormous undertaking, often requiring contradictory skills and actions such as adherence to a plan in tandem with solution-minded and outside the box critical thinking. This book examines the process of project management. Project management is the action of bringing all of a project's components together in an organized and efficient manner. This includes meeting established and agreed upon budgets and timeframes and ensuring that resources are handled appropriately. A variety of methods are currently in practice to produce consistent results, each with fundamental strengths and weaknesses. Ultimately, informed members of management should decide on the best fit.

| 1 |
The Traditional Approach

Project management was not a legitimate career path or defined competency until the mid-20th century. The management of projects has always been necessary, however, and project management as a concept has always been practiced, if only informally. Project management starts with a project. A project is an endeavor that is defined by a timeframe and a desired result. Since a project's duration is finite, its scope must also be finite. Because a project has a desired outcome it is also unique, set apart from routine activities. This logic distinguishes the field of project management from the world of regular operational management. Projects come in all shapes and sizes. Applied project management often begins when a new product is introduced to the market. Normal activities are initiated around the new product, and there is no need for more market preparedness, therefore the project is closed. Construction projects are also an example of a set of activities that is temporary and unique. Once the project is initiated it will take time until the bridge is built or the building is erected; when the construction is complete there are no longer any construction activities needed.

Expert management skills are absolutely essential to ensure that all activities and operations work smoothly and efficiently together, that deadlines are met, and that resources are used appropriately. Projects can include a virtually endless number of obstacles that can be inimical to the desired outcome. Project management then is defined as the process of planning, organizing, motivating, and controlling all relevant procedures, protocols, and resources to realize a project's specific goals. The Project Management Institute (PMI) divides the project management process into five distinct activities, which form the basis of the traditional approach to project management.

The traditional approach, synonymous with the software world's "waterfall method" works well for small and well-defined projects. Projects that require consideration of ever-changing needs or that take place in a highly dynamic environment (software development for example) are often a poor fit for the traditional project management approach. Not all projects will include all of the above five processes as projects can be terminated prior to completion and many processes will revisit the planning, executing, and monitoring and controlling phases throughout the project's lifecycle.

Project Initiation

Project initiation is the decision to begin a project, usually in response to a need. Project initiation can come from a variety of sources and circumstances. Reductions in market share or a competitor's release could spur a project focused on bringing a new product to the market. Rising property values in a suburban neighborhood could initiate a residential construction project. Any circumstances in which normal business activities don't fulfill an organization's needs could bring about a new project.

The initiation phase is also a time to identify critical parameters for the project's development including methods of communication, business cases, terms of quality, early visible risks, and specific goals. A review of current operations is also necessary during the project initiation phase to determine if a proposed project is viable or possible. This, in tandem with a stakeholder analysis, determines if there are sufficient resources available to achieve the outlined goal.

These defining project elements lay the groundwork for all future project activity. A vaguely defined scope or poorly assessed financial analysis could set a project in motion that has little to no real chance of success. An incomplete understanding of project goals and desired outcomes could mean that, come project close, too many open items persist and initial goals remain unmet. When initiating a project and determining objectives and scope, a proven standard to use is the SMART approach outlined below. Checking each objective against this system ensures that not only are objectives standardized and therefore easier to communicate and duplicate but that they are also realistic and measurable. The concept of SMART goals extends past the initiation process and can be applied to goals at all levels of the project lifecycle. SMART goals can also be applied to a multitude of other business applications and are a powerful enough concept to spill over into goal-setting at the personal level.

Project Planning

Planning is a critical component of a project lifecycle. Here the project's scope is defined in terms of deliverables, and the appropriate methods within that scope are identified to bring the project to a satisfactory close. Planning teams are selected and they produce the information needed to estimate schedules, costs and budget, resource requirements, required activities and their durations, and identification of specific goal-oriented deliverables. Flowcharts, schedules, and Gantt charts *(see fg. 1)* are generated within this phase to plan the execution of the project as well as to assess project progress further down the road within the project's lifecycle.

S	SPECIFIC – Well-defined
M	MEASURABLE – Tracked Progress
A	ACHIEVABLE – Can be Completed
R	REALISTIC – Reflect Resources
T	TIME-BOUND – Meet Deadlines

Workloads, teams, team leaders, and group effort assessments are also generated within this portion of the project lifecycle. Work breakdown structures *(see fg. 2)* and other means of assessing deliverables map the way to larger project goals by way of many, smaller goals. Because project planning happens at the outset of a project, many project aspects are unknown and many variables have yet to even be identified. Therefore the duration and effort estimations for project elements are often divided into optimistic, normal, and pessimistic cases. Each of these case types represents different effort and duration calculations based on possible project phase outcomes. Because of the uncertain nature of many projects, a margin of "safety time" is often factored into planning. Safety time represents a buffer of flexible time that is designed to account for unforeseen circumstances. Optimistic cases are instances in which very little safety time is needed, and the project will likely be completed ahead of schedule. Pessimistic cases are instances in which the safety time is insufficient to meet the needs of the project and completion by established deadlines is jeopardized.

OPTIMISTIC CASES	PESSIMISTIC CASES
• Reflect highly efficient use of time and resources.	• Reflect poor use of time and resources.
• Assume little interference of unforeseen variables.	• Assume high interference of unforeseen variables
• Provide desired level of project performance.	• Worst-case scenario
• Best-case scenario	• Normal cases fall between the two cases in severity and efficiency

All of these components of the planning process must be defined within themselves. Not all planning tools are created equal, and the wide range of project diversity mirrors the range of possible planning methods. "Scope creep" occurs when the features and scope of a project increase steadily during the project due to poor definition at the outset. If, in an effort to please stakeholders, the growth of a project is not controlled, scope creep can quickly out pace the available resources. Common issues such as scope creep underscore the importance of a thorough, well-documented, and well-defined project planning phase as well as the importance of strong risk planning.

Project Execution

Project execution is the direct implementation of the project plan. This phase of the project lifecycle puts resources into action and anticipates and produces the deliverables. The execution phase works hand-in-hand with project monitoring and control. Through execution, a project progresses along its lifecycle, headed toward closing. During this phase unforeseen changes crop up, risks are assessed, and budgets and timelines are challenged. The execution process must be measured and controlled in effective ways to ensure that timelines and budgets are kept in check.

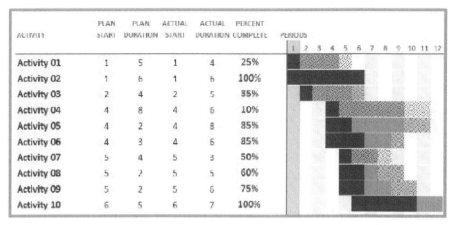

ACTIVITY	PLAN START	PLAN DURATION	ACTUAL START	ACTUAL DURATION	PERCENT COMPLETE	PERIODS
Activity 01	1	5	1	4	25%	
Activity 02	1	6	1	6	100%	
Activity 03	2	4	2	5	35%	
Activity 04	4	8	4	6	10%	
Activity 05	4	2	4	8	85%	
Activity 06	4	3	4	6	85%	
Activity 07	5	4	5	3	50%	
Activity 08	5	2	5	5	60%	
Activity 09	5	2	5	6	75%	
Activity 10	6	5	6	7	100%	

fg. 1 : A Gantt chart tracking ten activities measured over the duration of twelve periods. The darker solid segments represent planned effort and duration, the hatched portions actual effort and duration. The lighter solid portions represent percent completion past what was planned.

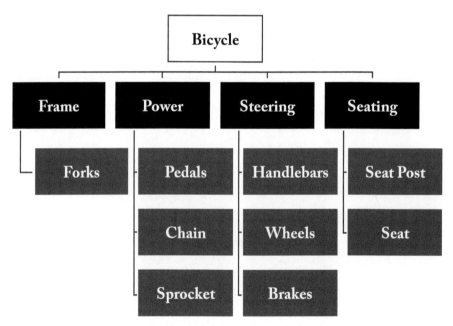

fg. 2 : A work breakdown structure for the production of a bicycle. Note that each level 2 (black) component is comprised of one or more level 3 (gray) components. For small projects with limited scope a simple list of tasks can often suffice in place of a detailed WBS.

Project Monitoring & Controlling

Because project execution is not an open-loop implementation, project monitoring is essential to overcoming unforeseen circumstances, tracking progress, and adhering to the plans developed in the project planning phase. Strict adherence to the project's plan can help prevent scope creep. Project control is included in this phase because monitoring alone will not ensure delivery of the desired results. Project control means using all available tools and resources to correct the trajectory of a project gone awry or to prevent the divergence from the project plans. Using proven monitoring best practices will also alert project managers when a project is in danger of failing to meet deadlines or running over-budget. Some key elements to include in project monitoring activities:

Measuring ongoing activities

Measure ongoing activities to establish a point of reference and build an accurate picture of where current activities lie within the project timeline.

Monitoring variables against the project plan

Monitor variables to identify when the project is at risk of diverting from the established projection. Key variables to monitor include costs, effort, resources, and scope.

Identifying corrective methods to properly overcome issues and risks

Indentify corrective methods to properly overcome issues and risks to ensure that if the project strays from the prescribed path, effective and direct methods exist to bring project performance in line with overall goals.

Ensuring that only approved changes are implemented

Ensure that only approved changes are implemented to limit scope creep and unauthorized project changes. This means using anticipating, identifying, and controlling methods to subvert the current authorization system. Unauthorized project changes can distract and divert progress away from the desired result and increase the risk of failure to meet deadlines or budgets.

Project monitoring is not a one-time activity; it is an ongoing process that consists of continuous feedback and support, correction of emerging errors, and updates to scope, budgets, and resources. This is not to say that change is hazardous to the health of a project; change is normal, expected, and inevitable. Ignoring the fact that change is a part of the project process can mean disastrous results if project activities are not monitored. Project monitoring and control is a cyclical activity. Activities, operations, and progress are measured to establish a baseline point of reference. These measurements are then compared to projected levels of activity and progress. If the measurements do not meet expectations, then corrective action is identified and implemented to bring progress back on track. Now that corrective action has been applied, the project's progress is again measured to verify the effectiveness of the corrective action, and the cycle begins again.

CORRECT

EVALUATE

MEASURE

The following list demonstrates some tools a project manager can use to asses the progress and health of a project:

- Investment analysis
- Cost-benefit analysis
- Value benefit analysis
- Expert surveys
- Simulation calculations
- Risk-profile analysis
- Milestone trend analysis
- Cost trend analysis

These methods and others track and evaluate key performance indicators (KPIs) that signal the project's direction and cohesion.

Project Closing

Project closing is the formal ending of a project's lifecycle. It is a reflective phase with important implications for future projects because lessons learned are archived and best practices are aggregated.

The project closing phase often consists of a post implementation review, which is an assessment of what went right as well as what went wrong. Understanding how staffing and workforce deployment contributed to a project's success (or failure) is essential for future undertakings. The process of contract closure is also a project closing phase activity. Contract closure is an administrative function that formally concludes professional contracts associated with the project lifecycle and examines and resolves any remaining open items.

Why Projects Fail?

The traditional project management approach represents the basic method for controlling and executing a project. Other options exist, each with a unique approach to increasing success rates and defined risks for project failure such as conforming to a budget or a schedule. Statistics vary as to the rate of failure among projects, but even conservative estimates are alarmingly high. The American Management Association

(AMA - *www.amanet.org*) outlines several key reasons that many organizations see projects end in failure.

1. Projects are not defined clearly at the executive level

This poor definition among decision-makers often stems from the lack of an agreement or consensus from top-level management. It can result in, as well as arise from, an informal or vague method of prioritizing projects, tasks, and resources. Scope creep is a common symptom of poor executive project definition, too, and changes that occur as a result will often lack the appropriate resources. The clearest way to protect against this obstacle is through communication and planning. Ensuring that comprehensive and thorough plans are in place locks down the roles of management, the tools to be used for execution, tracking, and controlling, and ensures that project resources are available.

2. Implementation plans are not team-developed

Without a cohesive and cooperative team assessment of project implementation, tasks of varying importance can be missed or under-valued. Poor communication can also cause to teams to overlook the interdependent nature of tasks, which can have disastrous results come project execution. These issues can be overcome through team planning and collective decision-making environments in which all roles and deadlines are clearly defined.

3. Stakeholders & management have unrealistic expectations

The best software in the world is limited by inputs and logic. A poorly planned project cannot rely on a software tool to pick up all of the planning "slack". A poor choice of software to handle project management needs can create issues in the long run as well. Software is meant to reduce the effort it takes to manage data, so If inputting data and keeping the system current requires more effort than using the software then it's a poor match. Making an informed decision at the outset of the project planning phase is a key element in the software selection process. Good channels of communication are essential to ensuring that all relevant decision makers and stakeholders understand the uses and limitations of each option. Additionally, when selecting software tools, it is important for organizations to have plans in place should the program fail, either in the form of support staff or alternative project management tools, or both.

4. Mismanagement

Unsurprisingly, poor management is a large culprit behind a project's failure. The blanket term "poor management" can be translated into several specific supervisory shortcomings. The first of these is a workload overload, or teams pursuing too many tasks or involved in too many projects. Some fields and management methods rely heavily upon cross-functional team members, but if team members move too often or are frequently pulled away from a team, project progress may suffer. Middle management staff often make the incorrect assumption that team members already know how to work efficiently in teams. This leads to surprises down the road when teams are inefficient or have poor progress levels. Training and team-based workshops on the front-end can save significant headaches on the back-end. Mismanagement doesn't stop at the team and middle management level; senior level management can also be guilty. Senior management that resists looking at project progress honestly and completely can stunt progression and can force issues to go unaddressed. Additionally, senior management that adopts a "just get it done" attitude can compromise quality and project integrity. Again, if issues remain unresolved, then facing the consequences down the road may be more difficult than addressing problems preemptively when they are discovered.

Because of the high rate of project failure within business organizations, alternative project management methods emerged. The following chapters discuss and outline various alternative methods of project management.

| 2 |

The Critical Chain Approach

Critical Chain Project Management (CCPM) focuses on the resources required to execute project activities and tasks. Differing from more rigid resource based methods, CCPM works to remain flexible while maintaining a level resource load. Start-time flexibility is a large component of CCPM that works to keep projects on schedule. This alternative to traditional project management has been attributed with speedy, cost-effective project completion. It is not uncommon for projects to run over schedule, cost more than budgeted, and exhaust resources; CCPM is designed to correct these prevalent issues.

The Theory of Constraints

CCPM is based on the Theory of Constraints (TOC). TOC asserts that every manageable system is limited in goal achievement based on the number of constraints affecting that system. A constraint is anything that prevents or impedes a system from achieving its goal. While there may be many hurdles and obstacles, the TOC tracks the sources of these hindrances back to their root causes, which are actually only a small number of constraints. The 5 Whys investigation method, outlined below, is used to identify the root cause of a problem. While not all problems will require five iterations of investigation, and others may require more, five is the agreed-upon average number for a thorough investigation.

Problem : There is a large amount of spoiled goods in a freezer.

Why 1 : Why are the goods spoiled?

Answer : Goods are spoiled when the temperature in the freezer rises above 0°C.

Why 2 : Why did the temperature rise above 0°C?

Answer : The freezer's operations malfunctioned allowing the temperature to rise.

Why 3 : Why did the freezer malfunction?

Answer : Goods stacked inside the freezer inhibited circulation and cut off the proper airflow needed to maintain the set temperature.

Why 4 : Why were goods stacked in this manner?

Answer : Operations have required an increasing amount of perishable frozen goods to be kept on hand.

Why 5 : Why are the excess goods not stored elsewhere to allow the freezer to function properly?

Answer : There are no other available freezers.

From this example the company can see that to continue operations at their current pace, additional freezer space is necessary to prevent further goods from spoiling in the future. The Theory of Constraints assumes that there will always be at least one constraint present within a given system. The TOC concept uses a focused process to identify each constraint in turn. Once the constraint is identified as a hindering force, the organization can structure corrective measures all the way up to total organizational restructure if necessary. This methodology is a practical application of the phrase "a chain is no stronger than its weakest link." No matter how strong a chain may be, one weak link can break it.

Once the goal of a system has been determined and measurements have been defined, the process is as follows:

1	Identify the constraint(s) associated with the system.
2	Determine how to eliminate the identified constraint(s)
3	Subordinate all other decisions to the above decision(s)
4	Elevate (expand) the system's constraints.
5	There is always at least one constraint impeding a system. Go back to step 1

The TOC process is a cycle of continuous improvement. As constraints are identified and the system is elevated, the efficiency of the output will increase.

The Critical Chain Process

In the world of project management, the critical chain is the sequence of terminal elements that are both precedence- and resource-dependent and prevent a project from being completed in time. Terminal elements are considered the lowest elements in the work breakdown structure and are not further subdivided in terms of effort, resources, and time. Referring back to *fig. 2* within this text, the deliverables rendered in grey represent terminal elements for the construction of a bicycle. This does not mean that there are not component processes involved with the production of such deliverables as "pedals" or "brakes," but simply put they are too detail-oriented for the overall work breakdown structure of bicycle assembly. A work breakdown structure is produced down to a specific level of interest. In the production of an aircraft, for example, the WBS may include installation of seating as a deliverable but not the production, sourcing, and transport of the seating. These processes are the responsibility of other assigned parties who have their own specific and detailed WBS regarding the assembly and production of the aircraft seating.

The difference between CCPM and other project management methods is how uncertainty within a project is managed. The critical chain links the deliverables that restrict a project's completion. The work structure for each deliverable embeds a certain amount of planned safety time. This safety time is often not explicitly expressed and is therefore "hidden" from the normal planning process.

CCPM planning combines hidden amounts of safety time into individual buffers. These buffers exist to protect projects from such pitfalls as bad multitasking and poor synchronization. Additionally CCPM addresses issues that arise from the human factor in many projects, namely Student Syndrome, Parkinson's Law, and task cherry picking. Student Syndrome is procrastination - the postponement of tasks until the last moment. Parkinson's Law occurs when project members delay or pace task completion to the point that it has an adverse effect on the project's completion. Cherry picking of tasks occurs when project members only undertake tasks that are easy, convenient, or in their comfort zones. Task cherry picking can have a highly adverse effect on the success of a project if tasks that are undesirable but critical are neglected.

CCPM's methodology reduces the aforementioned issues and protects planned safety time, which in turn protects project deadline adherence, and safety time that is included in the estimations for each task is "removed" and placed into aggregates known as buffers. Buffers are inserted into the project lifecycle at strategic points, divided into three critical areas that provide padding for the project's schedule adherence. These "time pools" protect against uncertainty and are consumed as tasks run past schedule. A general rule when implementing buffers is to remove 50% of the estimated time that is provided for each task or deliverable. This provides the aggregate of time that is re-divided into the buffers that are reinserted into the critical chain.

PROJECT BUFFER
- Inserted between the last task and the project's close.
- Delays originating from the project's longest chain consume this buffer.
- Recommended to be 50% safety time removed from project.

FEEDING BUFFERS
- Inserted between the last task on a feeding path and the critical chain.
- Delays that feed the longest chain consume this buffer.
- Recommended to be 50% the safety time removed from the feeding path.

RESOURCE BUFFERS
- Parallel to the critical chain.
- Ensure available resources match critical chain needs.
- Consumption of resources past budgets consumes this buffer

The buffer management method measures the amount of consumption of each buffer relative to project progress. The value of this measurement demonstrates the impact that delays have on delivering project objectives on the specified delivery date. Ideally, project tasks and activities will consume the established buffer at the same rate as they progress, resulting in a buffer that is completely consumed at a project's close. There are a variety of corrective actions that can be implemented if the buffer is consumed faster than project tasks and activities. It is the role of the project manager to 'recover' lost buffer time and bring the project back on track.

CCPM affects the execution phase by assigning priorities to resources or resource bundles. Tasks that affect the health of the critical chain are often assigned higher priority than tasks that serve to complete feeding tasks. Tasks throughout the entire critical chain are encouraged to use the 'roadrunner' method, which is the quickest progression of available project tasks (without compromising quality) before approaching the next task. This implementation reduces delays and errors caused by ineffective multitasking. The way in which project management and staff view the completion of a project is different as well. The remaining duration of tasks is emphasized and measured, not the percentage portion already completed. During monitoring and controlling activities if a project manager sees "days to complete" reports plateauing, becoming static, or increasing, then corrective action is necessary to protect buffer consumption and ensure timeliness of project delivery.

Criticisms

While CCPM strives to reduce errors and maintain a level load of resources, the project management method does suffer some criticisms. CCPM utilizes an as-late-as-possible scheduling method, which delays the start of work so that tasks are completed as close as possible to the project's target end date, contrasted to traditional approaches that aim to complete tasks as close as possible to the project's start date. This does have benefits; costs are incurred later in the project's lifecycle, and the critical early stages of the project are light on tasks, therefore the subject of higher focus. The detrimental side to this style of scheduling, however, is that all tasks become immediately critical for completion once a time threshold is reached. At later stages of the project lifecycle, any delays can affect completion within the deadline, and many critical tasks scheduled tightly against the project's deadline can be disastrous for adherence to time constraints. This characteristic of critical chain management underscores the importance of accurate and well-monitored buffers. The insertion of buffers into the project at the determined points is designed to absorb the effects uncertainty can have on the project in its final stages.

CCPM's method of task estimation is also a subject of criticism. The buffer system is only effective if the system is acclimated to seeking out that hidden safety time. It is not uncommon for project staff to rely on safety time or to be wary and cautious of its removal. Resistance to the method can dissolve somewhat with training. Emphasizing that the time is not 'going away' but is in fact being put into a bank or a pool that is redistributed across the project's chain is essential.

CCPM, like a great many organizational tools, requires support and commitment from the organization and its culture to thrive and provide optimal benefits. Within a wide range of business practice applications, indifferent management, uneducated staff, and inappropriate application cause new methods to fail.

| 3 |

Benefits Realization Management

Benefits realization management (BRM) is a traditional project management variant that is popular in the UK. The BRM method aligns project outcomes with overall business strategies, and this methodology has gained traction outside the United Kingdom to enjoy use in a variety of countries and industries. The BRM method is used to ensure that organizational benefits are the focus during continuing business operations. The program also focuses on outcomes, defined here as changes that are important to stakeholders within a particular project. Outcomes are divided into two categories: strategic and non-strategic. Strategic benefits, also known as "hard" benefits, are highly measurable. This includes benefits relating to cost or time savings. Non-strategic benefits, or "soft" benefits, are often intangible benefits that are difficult to measure. Benefits within this system are defined as the measurable positive impacts of change. A dis-benefit is a measurable negative impact of change.

The BRM system is based around the need for three things:

- Accountable People
- Relevant Measures
- Proactive Management of the benefits realization process

These three critical components work in tandem with BRM's three basic assumptions:

The creation of benefits is not a passive activity.

Benefits don't "automatically happen" when new methods or technologies are delivered. A benefits stream flows as the organization and staff become accustomed to it.

Benefits rarely happen according to plan.

Benefits cases are little more than estimates and must be monitored and checked frequently to ensure that outcomes are in line with expectations.

Benefits realization is not a onetime activity.

The realization of benefits is a cycle of implementation, results verification, and dynamic corrective activities as need be.

Without realizing it, many organizations and project managers may already be utilizing a benefits realization process. This process is passive or informal, however, it lacks understanding and refinement. The goal of BRM is to define, control, and optimize the benefits realization process.

The basic BRM process is outlined as follows:

1. Identify the investment outcomes.

- This includes defining benefit measures for each outcome.

- It also includes the collection of current benefit measures data to determine a benchmark and quantitative process for decision-making.

2. **All relevant parties and stakeholders must agree to a tailored BRM approach for the investment (project) in question.**

3. **Based on the BRM approach, project planning is necessary.**
   - This planning includes identifying new or changed capabilities needed to realize the established benefits.

   - This stage also includes planning the investments needed to enable the necessary changes for amended capabilities.

4. **Optimize the plan to reduce waste.**
   - This includes creating acceptable levels of resource consumption, risk, cost, quality, and time.

5. **Implement the plan.**
   - Throughout plan implementation, review is necessary to utilize gained insights and innovation for plan improvement.

6. **Once the plan is completed, monitoring is necessary to ensure that the BRM process continues to guarantee and sustain the benefits identified with the project.**

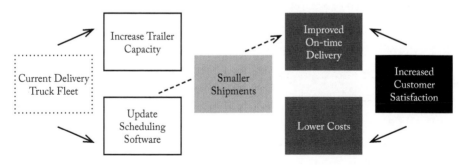

fg. 3 : A sample outcome map. The dotted outline level represents enablers, or existing states. The white level consists of enabling changes or changes that can bring about benefits. The light gray level shows the business changes that would be brought about through implementation of the enabling changes. The dark gray level represents benefits from the process, and the black level is the overall objective.

To aid decision makers and to identify investment outcomes, tools called outcome maps *(fg. 3)* are used. These visual representations are also known as results chains, benefits dependency networks, or benefit maps.

Benefits realization management was designed with efficient project execution in mind as well as a focus on aligning project tasks with the overall needs of the business. These concepts permeate the traditional project management process at both the initial planning stages and during the final stages of the project lifecycle. The outcome of the top-to-bottom influence is a collaborative and shared vision of the benefits realization process. This provides a clear picture to top-level management and project stakeholders of what results can be achieved through major investment. It also provides clear roles for middle management in the project execution process and the availability of resources.

Criticisms

BRM potentially falls victim to the communication-related issues that plague many project management and business systems. Within the benefits realization management structure specifically, a failure to clearly define desired benefits can start a project off on the wrong foot. Without a clear goal and scope, even the best-managed projects will fail to meet their marks while they search and play catch-up in the later stages of the project. This is related to setting unrealistic benefit targets. If an organization determines that costs should be cut by 50% within a particular operating sector, but the cost of doing business in that sector is rising by 15% annually, that goal may need to be reexamined or redefined.

| 41 |
Earned Value Management

Earned value management (EVM) measures performance and progress of a project objectively. This program combines three critical project characteristics (known as the project management triangle) into a single integrated system.

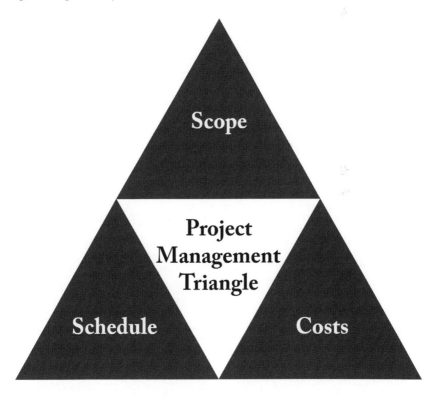

EVM has been successful in the areas of planning and control, scope definition, project performance analysis, surfacing and resolving contract disputes, and forecasting project performance issues.

EVM implementation relies on three critical features:

1. A project plan that identifies work to be accomplished.

2. A valuation of planned work known as Planned Value (PV) or Budgeted Cost of Work Scheduled (BCWS).

3. Predefined metrics known as "earning rules" used to quantify the accomplishment of work. Work is referred to within the system as Earned Value (EV) or Budgeted Cost of Work Performed (BCWP).

The basic premise of EVM quantifies progress using values for PV and EV. As project size increases, so does the number of indicators and factors needed for earned value management implantation; indicators and forecasts for cost performance and schedule performance are chief among these. EVM's application can be summed up with the following example.

A project has been approved for a duration of two years with a budget of $1M. Within the project planning phase it was determined that with proper progress the project would spend 50% of the approved budget within the first year. If project expenditures at the twelve-month mark are at or near $500,000, or 50% of the approved budget, the assumption is that the project is on track. The earned value management method challenges this assumption with the claim that budget expenditures alone do not provide sufficient information to determine the project's adherence to the plan. If the project has indeed spent 50% of the allotted budget at the one year mark, but only completed half of the work (25% of the total work) assigned to that portion of the budget, then the project has quite a bit of catching up to do. If the same $500,000 has been spent with 75% of the work completed, then the project is in fact ahead of schedule by 25%.

The missing component in the equation is earned value. EV is calculated using the following formula:

Earned Value (EV) = (Percent Complete) (Budget at Completion)

This formula measures project progress in the most objective manner possible. As EV tracks upward, so does progress completion. A standard EVM tracking graph plots planned value, actual cost, and earned value on the same graph for easy comparison of figures. *Fg. 4* is a sample EVM tracking graph. Areas in which the slope of the EVM curve is flat represent areas of little to no progress with the project. This metric is separate from budget expenditures because expenditures are not reliable indicators of progress. While monitoring budgets and project spending are important aspects of project management, under the EVM system the most important characteristic of a project is the accumulation of earned value.

The project outlined in *fg. 4* is a success. Not only are AC values lower than PV values, but EV is on the rise at all intervals with a brief exception near week six. It is important to note that even during this period of below-budget spending, the project is making little headway as EV dips slightly. This represents a week in which project progress is lower than normal even though spending is under budget. We can also extrapolate from the graph that although spending started off higher than expected, progress was still being made on the project albeit at a slow rate. As the slope of the EV curve increases, so does the project's efficiency. An AC value above the planned value line coupled with a low-slope EV is an undesirable position for project managers. This situation means that not only are costs overrunning the budget, but progress on the project is slow.

Standard EVM Tracking Chart

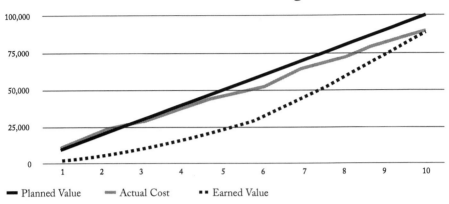

■ Planned Value　　　✄ Actual Cost　　　■ ■ Earned Value

fg. 4 : A sample of a typical EVM Tracking Chart that plots PV, AC, and EV on the same set of axes. The x-axis represents time measured in weeks; the y-axis is measured in dollars.

Calculations for EV may be made at a variety of intervals. These intervals are often determined during the project initiation phase but may change with the needs of the project. Possible intervals could either be monthly or weekly or could even be determined as progress is made. The project manager identifies each detailed component of completed work with a calculation of earned value and submits that report at each interval. The complexity of the EVM program depends heavily on the size and scope of the project at hand. While some companies have implemented EVM on only large-scale and complex projects, others are developing methods to scale the earned value management method for businesses of all sizes. This is a questionable approach for some as historically only massive projects have enjoyed notable benefits from wide-ranging EVM implementation. Implementation of EVM requires a minimum of three steps:

1. Define the work
2. Assign value
3. Define "earning rules"

Defining The Work

This is a basic component of project initiation. This is often done with a hierarchical chart such as a comprehensive work breakdown structure *(see fg. 2)*. This tree-like chart establishes a chain of mutually exclusive work segments that are easily defined and quantified.

Assigning Value

Assigning value determines the planned value (PV) for each task and activity. PV is an allotment of the total project budget and is often measured in currency, labor hours (effort), or both. This process is important because reaching a consensus on the weighted values of each activity and task solidifies understanding of the project's scope. Poor understanding of scope can lead to scope creep and running over-budget or behind schedule.

The Definition of Earning Rules

The definition of earning rules is a key element in tracking work in progress as well as measuring completed work. The simplest earning rule would be 0/100; no credit is earned for an activity until it is completed. Other popular options are 50/50 or 25/75. These earning rules provide partial credit upon activity initiation and the remainder upon completion. Once the plan is executed, these earning rules determine how EV is accumulated. Together, these stages provide the absolute minimum of planning required to undertake an EVM project.

Criticisms

Historically, EVM has suffered from being interpreted solely as a financial or accounting tool and not as an asset or integral part of the project management process. While it is true that the management style stemmed from financial origins, companies that have used EVM for large-scale projects with total commitment from staff throughout have had successful outcomes. Like CCPM, EVM requires commitment from top-level management as well as organizational support from a culture that understands and endorses the program. Any project that suffers from 'compliance fatigue' or a half-hearted attempt at participation is doomed to fail. Success can only be guaranteed through full commitment and support of the EVM process.

The earned value management process is a data-heavy project management method. No matter how accurate or efficient a calculator or formula is, its output is only as good as the numbers going in. Information comes from a number of sources - contractors, subcontractors, employees, auditors – and with a multitude of sources it is not difficult for information to become garbled or inaccurate. Software tools exist to aid earned value project managers. However, organizations should thoroughly examine all options before making a decision. A good software package that doesn't fit an organization's need is much more a liability than an asset.

Not only can data be incorrect, but there is also a massively large amount of it. Focusing on details simply because the data exists can produce a failure to spot larger trends, even if in retrospect it would have been easy to spot if project managers had been looking in the right place. Examining processes may be time consuming, but ensuring that the data used to make decisions and track progress is accurate is time well spent. When examining issues within the project, it is smart to focus not on 50 issues affecting deliverables, but instead on three or four critical issues. Working down the chain of priority keeps the project management teams from experiencing data overload.

Ensuring that contractors are also proficient in EVM application and methods is another critical method to stave off project pitfalls. The EVM method has attracted criticism with the number of contractors that claim to be experts with earned value management but cannot deliver a consistent level of service.

| 5 |
Agile Project Management

Agile project management is an iterative or incremental method of management. It is popular within the fields of engineering, information technology, and software development. These industries share a dynamic environment in which complex changes to a project's scope can happen frequently throughout a project's lifecycle. In this non-static project management environment rigid methods of management can have disastrous results. The following example outlines a situation in which Agile is the right project management choice.

A large manufacturer of widgets contracts a software development firm to produce new and purpose-built software that assists with production and distribution. The software will need to meet a series of requirements laid out by the widget manufacturer, and the project is scheduled to be completed within the year. Within that same year, the price of raw materials used for widget production skyrockets. The company is forced to find new suppliers who have different software integration needs than the suppliers that were on the books at the project's initiation. If the software development firm continues to produce the software as they have been contracted, the resulting product may have poor fitness for their clients.

Agile's iterative method produces incremental delivery of finished products so that the project's end goal is always in line with the needs of the customer. The widget manufacturer in the example would be as much a part of the process as the design team, and as a result all parties concerned can change project course as needed. In effect, the Agile method produces several smaller projects, each providing a client with a working deliverable. The client then provides feedback to the design team and has the option to continue the project or terminate it and accept the deliverables provided thus far.

Agile is based on the concept that three main notions of traditional project management are erroneous:

1. It is possible to plan a large project.
2. It is possible to protect against late changes.
3. It makes sense to lock in big projects early.

Agile management rejects these concepts based on the unpredictable nature of the project management environment. This is especially true for software design and development projects.

Agile has the following doctrines:

Individuals & Interactions	*over*	Processes & Tools
Working Software	*over*	Comprehensive Documentation
Customer Collaboration	*over*	Contract Negotiation
Responding to Change	*over*	Following a Plan

Agile practitioners don't claim that the methods on the right-hand side are without value, but this chart emphasizes that Agile values the methods on the left-hand more. As the name implies and as the items on the left show, Agile is a lightweight method of project management. The process eschews bureaucracy and extensive planning and instead favors small, nimble teams that collaborate with customers to anticipate and respond to change.

The 12 Principles of Agile Project Management

1. Our highest priority is to satisfy the customer through early and continuous delivery of valuable software.

2. Welcome changing requirements, even late in development. Agile processes harness change for the customer's competitive advantage.

3. Deliver working software frequently, from a couple of weeks to a couple of months, with a preference to the shorter timescale.

4. Business people and developers must work together daily throughout the project.

5. Build projects around motivated individuals. Give them the environment and support they need, and trust them to get the job done.

6. The most efficient and effective method of conveying information to and within a development team is face-to-face conversation.

7. Working software is the primary measure of progress.

8. Agile processes promote sustainable development. The sponsors, developers, and users should be able to maintain a constant pace indefinitely.

9. Continuous attention to technical excellence and good design enhances agility.

10. Simplicity – the art of maximizing the amount of work not done – is essential.

11. The best architectures, requirements, and designs emerge from self-organizing teams.

12. At regular intervals, the team reflects on how to become more effective, then tunes and adjusts its behavior accordingly.

The first principle focuses on the Voice of the Customer (VOC). While all projects are initiated out of a need of one kind or another, Agile focuses all project operation around the customer's needs. Hearing the VOC and working with customers on a daily basis is essential to aligning the project's goals with the customer's needs.

The next several principles outline the Agile process. Agile is based on collaboration with customers, responsiveness to a dynamic environment, and the iterative process. Agile management's focus on people is also evident within the 12 principles. Self-organization promotes quick response times and lightens the supervisory weight. With fewer 'veto-parties' or decision makers within the decision chain, emerging imperatives can be addressed more quickly. Less supervision also means less paperwork or process documentation, and self-organizing teams have all the information they need about their own capabilities and timeframes.

Though Agile is radically different from other conventional project management styles, the method still seeks to manage and control the same critical project factors. To reflect the dynamic environment of software development, scope is largely undefined. The total scope of a project is a background concept, but little immediate value is assigned to it. Instead, working segments of software are produced in iterations, or vertical slices. Since these are smaller components of a whole, their scope is easy to define. Once the slice is delivered to the customer, the customer's feedback directs the next iteration or slice. A plan that adheres to preconceived notions can lead the project astray and produce software that fails to meet the customer's needs. This is why practitioners of Agile claim it is nearly impossible for a well-executed Agile project to miss its mark; every step is approved by the customer, and the end product can be nothing other than exactly what the customer wants.

This adaptive project lifecycle also means that implementation and monitoring stages are also vastly different from traditional project management methods. While other management methods track progress toward a final goal, Agile methods use the production of working deliverables as the primary measures of progress. These vertical slices of the project represent complete phases of the project with their own scopes and goals. Since the entire direction of the overall project could change (or even be terminated) with the completion of each phase or iteration, more value is placed on the timely completion of these smaller phases.

Scrum

Scrum is a variation on the Agile methodology specifically aimed at the development and delivery of software. The name originates from a maneuver in the sport of Rugby in which each team uses its heaviest eight players in a pack to push the opposition's heaviest eight for control of the field. While Scrum is chiefly utilized to produce software, it has been stretched to fit other industries such as marketing.

Project initiation begins with a 'kick-off meeting,' and ends in 'sprints.' Sprints should be no longer than four weeks and strive to produce working deliverables at the end. Sprints start with a 'sprint-planning meeting' in which sprint goals are established and the team discusses staff roles and scope. If the sprint is not the first of the project, then the meeting will be combined with a 'sprint review meeting.' The purpose of a sprint review is to look back at progress and learn from mistakes or innovations. Throughout the sprint there are daily 'stand-up meetings,' so called because they are designed to be so short that sitting down would be irrelevant. These 15-minute meetings are designed to address key issues of productivity with the following questions:

- What did I do *yesterday* that was material to the sprint goal?
- What will I do *today* that is material to the sprint goal?
- Is there *anything stopping* us from reaching the sprint goal?

Throughout the project 'user-stories,' or customer needs expressed as features or functionality, are tracked using a tool called the task board *(fig. 5)*. A task board breaks user-stories down into tasks and tracks their status. A burndown chart *(fig. 6)* is used to track effort versus project completion. As effort is expended to complete tasks, the two metrics of completed tasks and remaining effort are plotted together with remaining tasks. It is considered a best practice method to post the burndown chart and task board where all associated team members can check them frequently.

SAMPLE TASK BOARD

STORY	NOT STARTED	STARTED	IN PROGRESS	DONE
USER STORY 1	H	F	B	A
	I	G	D	C
USER STORY 2	J			
	K		E	

fig. 5 : A sample task board. Task boards are effective progress tracking tools and should be posted in a traffic area where team members can review project progress frequently.

SAMPLE BURNDOWN CHART

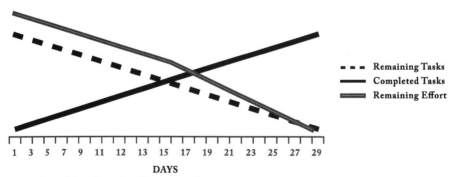

fig. 6 : A sample burndown chart. Remaining effort is plotted along with remaining tasks and completed tasks to track project progress.

The tasks required to complete the project are assembled into a project backlog. The tasks required to complete each sprint are assembled into a sprint backlog. User-stories are divided into backlog items with weighted effort estimations. True to the Agile method, Scrum projects utilize lightweight administrative staff. Within the Scrum method there are three primary roles:

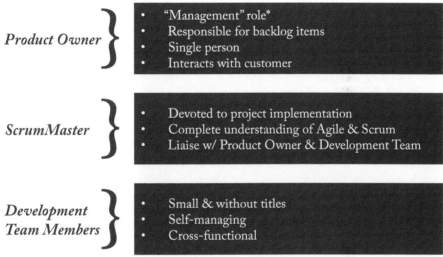

Product Owner
- "Management" role*
- Responsible for backlog items
- Single person
- Interacts with customer

ScrumMaster
- Devoted to project implementation
- Complete understanding of Agile & Scrum
- Liaise w/ Product Owner & Development Team

Development Team Members
- Small & without titles
- Self-managing
- Cross-functional

* While the Product Owner defies the normal definition of a manager, it is the position closest in responsibility to that of a conventional manager.

Within a Scrum project there may be many small, self-organizing development teams, but the ScrumMaster and Product Owner roles almost always belong to a single person respectively. One variation on the single-Product Owner system is a Product Owner Panel, or a group of project managers that collectively determine user-stories and backlog items. This is an unconventional approach to Scrum and often reflects a company's reluctance to adopt the Scrum methodology entirely. As with many organizational doctrines, incomplete adoption challenges the longevity of such programs, and commitment to a single method is usually the recommended course of action. Like all decisions, however, the best decision is an informed one.

The Product Owner coordinates the customer's desired features into "user-stories" and creates a task backlog for each. The Product Owner interacts with the customer frequently, on a daily basis if possible, and guides the project in the appropriate direction. The ScrumMaster often serves multiple teams simultaneously and facilitates the Scrum process. He or she removes impediments for the development teams and provides guidance to ensure that they are adhering to Scrum methods. The ScrumMaster also works to collectively define the "Done" status for tasks. This is a critical communication and progress tracking system. Development teams do the actual work to produce software. These teams are cross-functional, meaning that members may be shifted from one team to another as their expertise is needed. Development team members are all titled "developers." The teams are self-organizing and work to complete backlog items during sprints.

For a more in-depth look at the functionality and methodology behind the Scrum program, check out the Scrum QuickStart Guide: A Simplified Beginner's Guide to Mastering Scrum, another informative and comprehensive title from the Clyde Bank Media library.

Criticisms

A major criticism of Scrum, which extends to the entire Agile method, is that constant, daily customer inclusion in the development process is a lofty goal and is not always a reality. In too many cases customers find it difficult to articulate their own needs. In other cases, the customer simply doesn't have the resources to commit someone to interface with their software development account.

Additionally, many organizations have applied Scrum or Agile without thoroughly investigating the commitments that implementation entails. Scrum is a complex system that is radically different from other forms of project management. It requires extensive training for staff and management alike and requires adherence to the Scrum model to succeed. While knowledge is circulating more rapidly regarding the Agile stable of methodologies, misconceptions still abound. This coupled with the high cost of extensive training and workshops for staff has turned some companies off to the notion of Scrum development.

conclusion

Project management has been around since the beginnings of modern business, and it is here to stay. As the overlapping and interconnected spheres of the business world intersect in new and more complex ways, the role of project manager will also become more involved. While a bevy of project management methods exist, the best method is the one that makes sense for the project at hand. Understanding the fundamental strengths and weaknesses of each project management method is key to selecting the most appropriate method. A less than genuine commitment to any business model or practice can result in disaster. These management models have structure and rules for a reason; while every model is best stretched to fit an organization's particular needs, practitioners should be mindful of the basic tenets of each system's doctrine. A project manager who is willing to think outside the box and consider the full range of options stands apart from the crowd. Those who exhibit solution-minded responses, critical thinking, and a willingness to learn and explore will ultimately shape the directions of their organizations.

about clydebank

We are a multi-media publishing company that provides reliable, high-quality and easily accessible information to a global customer base. Developed out of the need for beginner-friendly content that is accessible across multiple formats, we deliver reliable, up-to-date, high-quality information through our multiple product offerings.

Through our strategic partnerships with some of the world's largest retailers, we are able to simplify the learning process for customers around the world, providing them with an authoritative source of information for the subjects that matter to them. Our end-user focused philosophy puts the satisfaction of our customers at the forefront of our mission. We are committed to creating multi-media products that allow our customers to learn what they want, when they want and how they want.

ClydeBank Business is a division of the multimedia-publishing firm ClydeBank Media LLC. ClydeBank Media's goal is to provide affordable, accessible information to a global market through different forms of media such as eBooks, paperback books and audio books. Company divisions are based on subject matter, each consisting of a dedicated team of researchers, writers, editors and designers.

For more information, please visit us at :
www.clydebankmedia.com
or contact *info@clydebankmedia.com*

notes

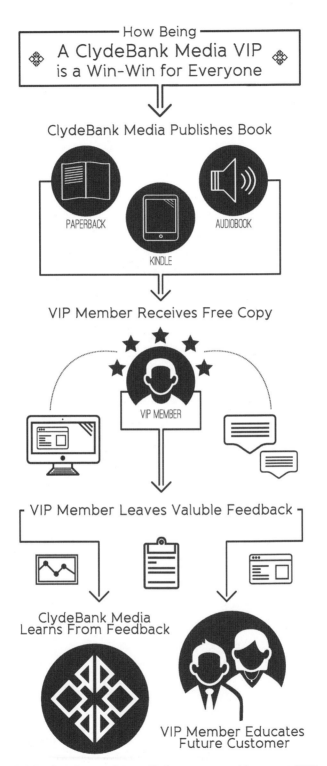

Visit *www.clydebankmedia.com/vip* to find out more and become a VIP member!

Get a *FREE* ClydeBank Media Audiobook
+ 30 Day Free Trial to Audible.com

Get titles like this absolutely free :

- *Business Plan Quickstart Guide*
- *Options Trading Quickstart Guide*
- *ITIL For Beginners*
- *Scrum Quickstart Guide*
- *JavaScript Quickstart Guide*
- *3D Printing Quickstart Guide*

- *LLC Quickstart Guide*
- *Lean Six Sigma Quickstart Guide*
- *Project Management QuickStart Guide*
- *Social Security Simplified*
- *Medicare Simplified*
- *and more!*

To Sign Up & Get your Free Audiobook, visit :
www.clydebankmedia.com/audible-trial

Printed in Great Britain
by Amazon